The Thinker's Toolbox

A Practical and Easy Approach to Creative Thinking

Pamela Thornburg

David Thornburg

DALE SEYMOUR PUBLICATIONS

Cover design: Rachel Gage
Cartoons: John Johnson

This book is published by Dale Seymour Publications®, an imprint of
Addison Wesley Longman, Inc.

Dale Seymour Publications
10 Bank Street
White Plains, NY 10602
Customer Service: 800-872-1100

Order number DS13900
ISBN 0-86651-467-8

7 8 9 10 11-ML-02-01-00-99-98

DALE
SEYMOUR
PUBLICATIONS®

To Ernest and Virginia Howe,
our parents and friends

Acknowledgments

We wish to express our appreciation to the Redwood City School District for granting Pamela a sabbatical leave to study thinking skills. Without that leave it is unlikely that this book would have been written. We are grateful to Linda Denman, principal of the John Gill School, for her encouragement and endless support. We also thank Superintendent Dr. Ken Hill and Assistant Superintendent Robert Beuthel of the Redwood City School District for their support.

Gini Shimabukuro is a close friend and supporter who acted as our unofficial editor. Words can scarcely express the depth of our appreciation for her heartfelt encouragement.

Thanks, too, to Dale Seymour for his vision and to Beverly Cory, our editor, whose keen sense of style has helped us transform our original ideas into a book we hope will benefit students and educators everywhere.

Like many educators, we know that our students are also our best teachers. To our past, present, and future students at the John Gill School and in the Design Division at Stanford University, we express our heartfelt thanks. In the final analysis, this book's for you.

Contents

Introduction   1

Part One • Introducing the Tools ———————————————— **5**

Eliminate   7

Elaborate   15

Describe   21

Combine   28

Rearrange   34

Classify   42

Substitute   50

Reduce   59

Exaggerate   67

Empathize   73

Compare   81

Associate   87

Hypothesize   94

Symbolize   101

Separate   108

Reverse   114

Part Two • Challenge Problems ——————————————— **123**

Thinker's Toolbox Challenge Problem Form   **124**

Using the Challenge Problems   **125**

Challenge Problems 1–59   **126**

Summary of Tools   **136**

Bibliography   **138**

Introduction

There is only one right answer to most of the problems we expect children to solve in school. For example, the problem "What number is midway between 3 and 7?" has only one right answer. If a student says "5," the answer is correct; any other response is incorrect.

While developing the ability to solve specific problems like this one is an essential component of education, it is equally important that we provide students with practical experience in solving real-world problems for which there may be an unlimited number of equally valid answers. For example, what is the best way to take a piano out of an apartment on the 30th floor when it won't fit in the elevator? The solutions to this problem can range from using a helicopter to lift it through the picture window to taking the piano apart and carrying it down in pieces. There is no single right or wrong answer to problems of this type—problems that are quite commonplace outside the classroom.

The solution of real-life problems often requires skills in *divergent thinking*, the ability to create numerous alternatives from which to choose a final solution. Divergent thinking skills can be taught, and much of the work in developing higher order thinking skills includes at least some focus on this important topic. The capacity for divergent thinking is separate from the linear, sequential thinking process we use when we solve a traditional math problem or recall a piece of information for a history examination. Divergent thinking is a cornerstone of the creative process.

Unfortunately, many of us find our creative thinking skills blocked from time to time, especially when we are confronted with a hard problem to solve. To see a real-life creative block in action, take a sheet of paper and list 100 uses for a ball-point pen. If you are like most people, you will find yourself blocked until you get past the idea of the pen as only a writing instrument.

While conceptual blocks are commonplace, there are ways to break through these blocks and to get the creative juices flowing again. *The Thinker's Toolbox* material you have in your hands provides a set of tools for breaking through such blocks.

The underlying idea of *The Thinker's Toolbox* is this: By thinking about a problem in light of a selected verb, such as *elaborate,* we can generate new ideas to help us solve the problem. This notion of problem solving as a verb is not a new one. It forms the basis of the SCAMPER problem-solving materials, created as an outgrowth of Alex Osborn's work in brainstorming.* James Adams, in his book

---

* See the bibliography on page 138 for a selection of materials on creative thinking.

The Care and Feeding of Ideas, lists several verbs that are useful as "set breakers," or words that can help generate ideas once the student starts to run out of steam. For *The Thinker's Toolbox* we have chosen sixteen verbs that together make up a practical, adaptable kit of tools for life-long problem solving.

A WORD OF CAUTION

A list of sixteen problem-solving verbs is hard to remember, and if the problem solver has to struggle to remember a technique for breaking through a conceptual block, that makes the problem even harder to solve. Therefore we recommend that students have a permanent list of these problem-solving verbs, and that they always be allowed to refer to the list to help them choose strategies when solving problems on their own. The "Summary of Tools" on pages 136-137 can be duplicated for such student use.

It is distinctly not our purpose to have students memorize the techniques in this book. Instead these materials, with their rich assortment of examples, are designed to give students practice in divergent thinking and facility in using the different tools.

The tools are to be used by students not just with the problems set forth in these pages, but whenever they find themselves blocked in the creative problem-solving process. The approach described in *The Thinker's Toolbox* is similar to methods used by business executives in their own creative problem solving. Thus students who experience these tools in your classroom will be learning a technique with immediate real-world applications.

USING THESE MATERIALS

The Thinker's Toolbox is divided into two parts. "Part One: Introducing the Tools" helps students explore the function and application of each of the sixteen tools. A teacher's overview for each tool gives you a description of the tool, examples of its use, and several applications for which this tool is appropriate. Notice that these applications range from concrete problems in the students' own everyday lives to more abstract, "adult" problems taken from the world outside the classroom. Following the overview is a blackline master for each given application that you can duplicate for classroom use.

In covering this material, allow plenty of time for group interaction on the problems. In this manner students will learn to "springboard" off of each other's ideas, and as a result the nature and excitement of divergent thinking will become obvious.

"Part Two: Challenge Problems" gives students a chance to apply what they have learned. It consists of more than 50 problems for which the students might use any tools of their choosing to generate alternative solutions. This section brings students closer to real-world problem solving as they experiment with different tools to find the ones that work for them in each new situation.

We say that this book is appropriate for grades 3 through 8. Some may argue that good instructional materials can't work for such a wide range. For some subjects that may be true, but not for divergent thinking. The problems in this book and the tools for solving them have been tackled by students as young as eight, as well as by engineers and designers from our nation's largest corporations. Give a third-grade class and an eighth-grade class the same problem, and they might generate quite different lists of possible solutions—but for both, the problem is guaranteed to be a challenge.

ANOTHER NOTE OF CAUTION

Creative ideas are as fragile as the petals of a rose. Just as frost can wilt a flower in minutes, cold water can dampen the flow of ideas to a mere trickle. As students provide alternative solutions to problems, be sure that judgment is suspended until all the ideas are captured. During the divergent phase of the problem-solving process, all ideas should be considered equally valid. Be careful neither to criticize nor to applaud any one idea. However, if you notice that the class has gotten into a rut, you can interrupt the idea-generating process to suggest that they look for a completely different approach.

Most ruts fall in the category we call "fluency traps." For example, if one solution to a problem is "paint it pink" and the students continue with "paint it red, blue, white," and so forth, they are demonstrating *fluency* within the domain of painted colors, but not *flexibility*—the ability to create completely new categories of solutions. Good problem solving requires both flexibility and fluency. While students can (and should) be warned about fluency traps, there is no substitute for your watchful ear and eye as ideas are generated.

REACHING CLOSURE

Even though the focus of this book is divergent thinking, problems are not solved until a final solution is chosen. Achieving closure in problem solving is as important as coming up with many possible solutions in the first place. However, because our school system has traditionally emphasized finding a "final" answer, students need much more practice in generating multiple options. That's why our focus in the first part of the book is on the divergent thinking process itself.

Once the class has generated a long list of potential solutions, then the convergent thinking process can start. At this point students can measure each suggested idea against the original problem to see if it is relevant, irrelevant, or interesting and worth looking at later. By separating the quest for an answer from the generation of possibilities, you will maintain an environment in which divergent thinking can thrive.

People who are new to this method of thinking are often surprised at the richness and sheer number of ideas they come up with. With this variety to choose from, the final solution chosen is bound to be a good one.

ABOUT GRADING

We prefer that the activities in this book not be graded. There are two main reasons for this. First, creative (divergent) thinking can be hampered by stress. If students think that their choices are going to be analysed and graded, they will tend to produce only predictable and clearly relevant ideas, rather than explore the problem domain freely. Second, it takes a tremendous amount of effort on the teacher's part to grade creative work without allowing a personal aesthetic sense or other subjective judgment to influence the grade. A generation ago, a child who suggested that we look to the moon as a source of raw materials might have been criticized (even "graded down") for impracticality, and yet today, ideas like this receive a lot of attention in the halls of our most successful industries. The child's capacity to imagine a future far different from our past should be encouraged, and we feel that this is best done in an ungraded setting.

If, for whatever reason, you find it necessary to grade your assignments in divergent thinking, we recommend that the grade be based on the following criteria:

- *The* quantity *and* quality *of ideas generated during the divergent thinking phase of the activity.* Be on the lookout for flexibility and fluency. Also, be aware that some children may generate hundreds of ideas for one particular problem and only a few ideas for another one.

- *The appropriateness of the solution(s) that the student feels would be worth trying out.* These choices need not be the conventional ones you might expect, but may be very ingenious. For example, when Karl Gauss was a child, his teacher asked him to add the numbers from 1 to 100 in an attempt to occupy his time. He produced the answer immediately by realizing that 1 + 100 was the same as 2 + 99; from this he was able to derive a simple equation that gave the result. Gauss went on to become one of the world's most important mathematicians.

- *The ability of the child to explain his or her reasons for making the final selection of the problem solution(s).* This metacognitive act is often left out, yet it is very important. Whether a student picks a solution because it is the least expensive, the prettiest, the most imaginative, the most likely to succeed, or for any other reason, the very act of thinking about the basis for the choice allows the student to develop an understanding of the subtle forces that lead us to make one choice over another. It is important that children be encouraged to articulate this process.

A FINAL NOTE
Creative thinking skills are important for everyone—including you. We recommend that you work on some of these assignments along with your students. We know that you will find the tools applicable to your own life, just as your students will find them applicable to theirs.

Pamela and David Thornburg
May 1988

PART ONE

Introducing the Tools

ELIMINATE

Teacher's Overview

NAME OF TOOL: Eliminate

DEFINITION: Omit; take away; get rid of.

DESCRIPTION: This tool enables the student to solve a problem by simplifying the situation, getting down to the very essence of the matter at hand. Sometimes a problem is a problem simply because there is a clutter of extraneous material, or more than can be comfortably handled. Such challenges can be solved by eliminating unessential components or assumptions.

APPLICATIONS

1. Your desk at school is too cluttered. What things could you eliminate to make it neat? Draw a "before" and "after" picture.

2. You are going on an airplane to spend a month at your cousin's house, and you have a list of twelve favorite belongings that you want to take with you. Your mother says you can take only four of them. Which ones do you eliminate? Make the list, then eliminate items until there are only four left. How did you make your choices? Draw a picture showing how you will pack these items for travel.

3. The 50 states are getting too hard to control. Which three would you eliminate? Why? Draw a map of the United States, leaving out the states you eliminated. Label the remaining states. Are there any problems with the map as a result of eliminating some states?

4. You are dressed up for a fancy party and your friend tells you that you are too dressed up. What would you eliminate to become more casual? Draw a "before" and "after" picture.

5. You are a parent with four children. You want to plan several enjoyable activities for them to do in one day, as a group. What activities would you choose? List the four activities and draw pictures of them. Next, you find that there isn't enough time to do all you have planned. Which activities would you eliminate? Why?

6. You are a designer of cars. The owner of the company isn't pleased with your latest design. He says there are too many distracting items on the car. What can you eliminate? Why? Draw the car as originally designed. Be as fancy as you like. Then draw the car again after you have eliminated some parts of the design. Which car looks the best to you? Share your pictures with a friend and ask which one he or she likes best.

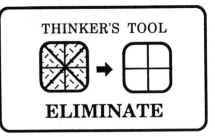

THINKER'S TOOL

ELIMINATE

Your desk at school is too cluttered.
What things could you eliminate to make it neat?

Draw a "before" and "after" picture.

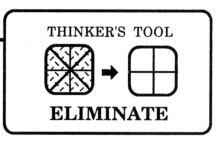

THINKER'S TOOL

ELIMINATE

You are going on an airplane to spend a month at your cousin's house, and you have a list of twelve favorite belongings that you want to take with you. Your mother says you can take only four of them. Which ones do you eliminate? Make the list, then eliminate items until there are only four left.

How did you make your choices?

Draw a picture showing how you will pack these items, along with your clothing, for travel. Label your picture.

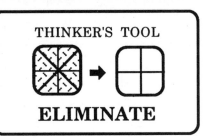

THINKER'S TOOL

ELIMINATE

The 50 states are getting too hard to control. Which three would you eliminate? Why?

Draw a map of the United States, leaving out the states you eliminated. Label the remaining states. Are there any problems with the map as a result of eliminating some states?

THINKER'S TOOL

ELIMINATE

You are dressed up for a fancy party and your friend tells you that you are too dressed up. What would you eliminate to become more casual?

Draw a "before" and "after" picture.

THINKER'S TOOL

ELIMINATE

You are a parent with four children. You want to plan several enjoyable activities for them to do in one day, as a group. What activities would you choose? List the four activities and draw pictures of them.

Next, you find that there isn't enough time to do all you have planned. Which activities would you eliminate? Why?

THINKER'S TOOL

ELIMINATE

You are a designer of cars. The owner of the company isn't pleased with your latest design. He says there are too many distracting items on the car. What can you eliminate? Why?

Draw the car as originally designed. Be as fancy as you like. Then draw the car again after you have eliminated some parts of the design. Which car looks the best to you? Share your pictures with a friend and ask which one he or she likes best.

ELABORATE

Teacher's Overview

NAME OF TOOL: Elaborate

DEFINITION: Add details; make something new by adding on to something already created.

DESCRIPTION: Sometimes a solution to a problem can be found by adding something new to an existing product or situation. For example, when personal tape players like the Sony Walkman first appeared, they were quite popular. As the market for these items reached a plateau, the product was elaborated upon by the addition of an AM/FM radio, thus creating a new product. New automobile designs are often elaborations on existing ideas. Edison improved the telephone by elaborating on the original microphone assembly and creating the carbon microphone cartridge used to this very day.

APPLICATIONS

1. The teacher will give you some basic sentences. You are to elaborate on each one, adding details to make it more descriptive. For example:

Basic sentence: The dog crossed the road.

Elaboration: The *shaggy black* dog *that Mrs. Elwood rescued from the pound* crossed the *busy* road *in a flash to save a crying baby.*

Possible basic sentences:

- The man cleaned the house.
- The teacher went to the movie.
- The girl ran.
- The ball flew into the street.
- The dinner got cold.

Choose your favorite two sentences and draw an illustration for each one.

2. Your teacher has assigned a six-page report on your state. You have written two pages, but now you're stuck. How are you going to expand your report to six pages? List as many ideas as you can.

3. You are a fashion designer creating clothes for the person who has very little money to spend. How could you elaborate on a basic black jacket to make it more interesting? What could you add? What could you make larger? What could you make smaller? What could you add to make it fancier? Draw a picture of the basic black jacket, then another picture showing your elaborations.

4. You own a paper clip company and you produced too many paper clips. The clips aren't selling. What could you add to them to make them more appealing? (For example, you could add a colored bead.) Brainstorm a list of things you could add to the paper clip. Draw each one. Which do you think would sell the best? Why?

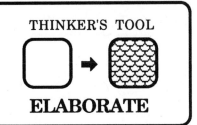

THINKER'S TOOL

ELABORATE

The teacher will give you some basic sentences. You are to elaborate on each one, adding details to make it more descriptive. Write the basic sentences below.

-
-
-
-
-

Write your elaborated sentences here:

-
-
-
-
-

Choose your favorite two sentences and draw an illustration for each one.

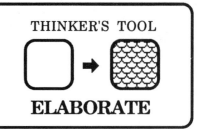

THINKER'S TOOL

ELABORATE

Your teacher has assigned a six-page report on your state. You have written two pages, but now you're stuck. How are you going to expand your report to six pages? List as many ideas as you can.

THINKER'S TOOL

ELABORATE

You are a fashion designer creating clothes for the person who has very little money to spend. How could you elaborate on a basic black jacket to make it more interesting?

What could you add?

What could you make larger?

What could you make smaller?

What could you add to make it fancier?

Draw a picture of the basic black jacket, then another picture showing your elaborations.

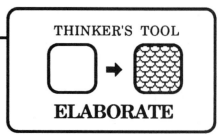

THINKER'S TOOL

ELABORATE

You own a paper clip company and you
produced too many paper clips. The clips
aren't selling. What could you add to them
to make them more appealing? (For example,
you could add a colored bead.)

Brainstorm a list of things you could add to the paper clip.

Draw each one. Which do you think would sell the best? Why?

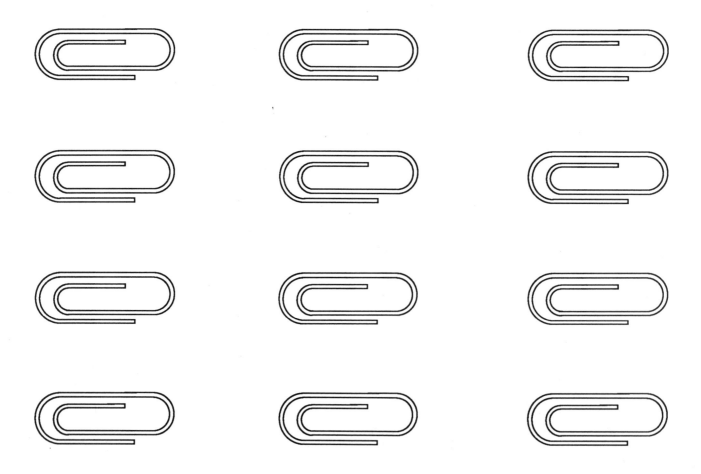

DESCRIBE

Teacher's Overview

NAME OF TOOL: Describe

DEFINITION: Give a picture in words.

DESCRIPTION: Some problems are made easier simply by describing them—by putting them into words. This is especially true for complex problems that may be presented in a non-verbal fashion. The act of expressing a problem in words can often lead to new insights that clarify and help generate solutions. For example, writers often "talk out" their basic ideas for a movie or novel and find that this process stimulates the flow of ideas. If we do the describing while someone else listens, the second person often has insights that are helpful to us in solving the problem.

APPLICATIONS

1. You would like to design a school desk that is more "user friendly," but you aren't sure what changes to make. Start by describing the standard desk in full detail. How tall is it? How wide is it? What is its color? Texture? Shape? Smell? When your description is complete, make notes for possible changes that would create a friendlier desk.

2. Your teacher, who has never met your parents, wants to be sure to talk to them after the parent volunteer meeting tonight. Describe your mother or father so they couldn't be mistaken for someone else. Draw a picture to help your teacher, and compare the picture with your description.

3. Describe yourself to a pen pal you've never met. Draw a picture of yourself to go along with your written description.

---

4. Describe the color red to a friend who cannot see. (Hint: Does the color red correspond to any feelings, tastes, smells, or sounds?) Describe the color blue to the same person. Describe a glorious sunset in a way that will make your blind friend feel its beauty.

5. Think of someone who has been bugging you lately. Without naming names, tell what this person has been doing that irritates you. Describe at least three different examples of this behavior. Does the person seem to know how much these actions bother you? Do other people seem to be bothered, too?

ADDITIONAL ACTIVITY

Have each student draw a picture of a simple object—such as a tree, a flower, a dog—on a sheet of drawing paper. Each student must then describe in written detail how to draw this picture so that another student can reconstruct it from the written description. Details should include color, size, shape, placement on the page, and so forth.

Have the students compare the drawings made from the written descriptions with the original drawings and note the results. Is it hard to describe pictures in words?

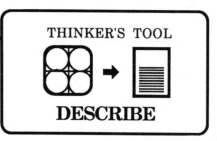

THINKER'S TOOL

DESCRIBE

You would like to design a school desk that is more "user friendly," but you aren't sure what changes to make. Start by describing the standard desk in full detail. How tall is it? How wide is it? What is its color? Texture? Shape? Smell?

When your description is complete, make notes for possible changes that would create a friendlier desk.

THINKER'S TOOL

DESCRIBE

Your teacher, who has never met your parents, wants to be sure to talk to them after the parent volunteer meeting tonight. Describe your mother or father so they couldn't be mistaken for someone else.

Draw a picture to help your teacher and compare the picture with your description.

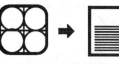

THINKER'S TOOL

DESCRIBE

Describe yourself to a pen pal you've never met.

Draw a picture of yourself to go along with your written description.

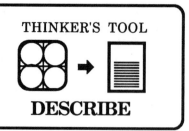

THINKER'S TOOL

DESCRIBE

Describe the color red to a friend who cannot see. (Hint: Does the color red correspond to any feelings, tastes, smells, or sounds?)

Describe the color blue to the same person.

Describe a glorious sunset in a way that will make your blind friend feel its beauty.

Using a Tool from the Thinker's Toolbox

THINKER'S TOOL

DESCRIBE

Think of someone who has been bugging you lately. Without naming names, tell what this person has been doing that irritates you. Describe at least three different examples of this behavior.

Does the person seem to know how much these actions bother you? Do other people seem to be bothered, too?

COMBINE

Teacher's Overview

NAME OF TOOL: Combine

DEFINITION: Join or put things together.

DESCRIPTION: Numerous inventions are the result of combining two known things to create something completely new. The combination of erasers with pencils took place so long ago that we might think pencils were always made this way—but it isn't true. This combination made pencils much easier to carry and use. The combination of peanut butter and celery creates a delicious snack. The combination of a radio and a clock created the clock radio, allowing people to awaken to music instead of an alarm bell.

APPLICATIONS

1. Using a dictionary, pick a word at random by naming two numbers—first a page number, then a word number. *(TEACHING NOTE: Before the students pick their numbers, find the range for each type of number by counting the words on a typical page of your classroom dictionary and noting how many pages the dictionary has.)* Turn to the page number you have selected and count down to the selected word. This is your first word. Repeat this process to choose a second word. When you have selected two words, list all the ideas that come to mind when you join these two words together.

For example, suppose the two words were *cab* and *noticeable*. You might create a *noticeable cab* by painting it bright purple, putting a neon sign on the roof, or installing a musical horn. What other associations can you make for these two words? Can you use them to create new inventions? Now choose two other words and combine them for a new invention.

2. You have been asked by a toy company to design a new bicycle for kids. What things could you join together to create a new bike? For example, could you attach a skateboard to the rear axle? What could you add to the fenders, pedals, wheels, or handlebars? How would combining things make the bike more versatile, more enjoyable, or otherwise more marketable?

3. You are the president of a fruit juice company and your sales are slipping. What two ingredients could you combine to create a brand new drink? For example, could you make an apple-bubblegum flavored juice? List all your ideas for new combinations. Create an advertisement for your favorite combination.

4. You have invited eight friends for dinner tonight and they have already tasted most of your dishes. What recipes could you combine to create a completely new meal? For example, you could combine lasagne and spaghetti to make *lasghetti*. This would be lasagne sauce on spaghetti, topped with cheese and baked in the oven. As another example, you could combine clam chowder and chicken soup to make ocean-chicken chowder.

How many combinations can you come up with? Create an advertisement for your favorite new recipe and draw a picture of your creation.

THINKER'S TOOL

COMBINE

Using a dictionary, pick a word at random by naming two numbers—first a page number, then a word number.

Turn to the page number you have selected and count down to the selected word. This is your first word. Repeat this process to choose a second word. When you have selected two words, list all the ideas that come to mind when you join these two words together. What other associations can you make for these two words? Can you use them to create new inventions?

Now choose two other words and combine them for a new invention.

THINKER'S TOOL

COMBINE

You have been asked by a toy company to design a new bicycle for kids. What things could you join together to create a new bike? For example, could you attach a skateboard to the rear axle? What could you add to the fenders, pedals, wheels, or handlebars?

How would combining things make the bike more versatile, more enjoyable, or otherwise more marketable?

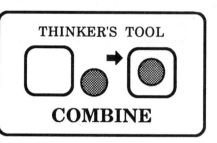

You are the president of a fruit juice company and your sales are slipping. What two ingredients could you combine to create a brand new drink? For example, could you make an apple-bubblegum flavored juice? List all your ideas for new combinations.

Create an advertisement for your favorite combination.

You have invited eight friends for dinner tonight and they have already tasted most of your dishes. What recipes could you combine to create a completely new meal? For example, you could combine lasagne and spaghetti to make *lasghetti*. This would be lasagne sauce on spaghetti, topped with cheese and baked in the oven. As another example, you could combine clam chowder and chicken soup to make ocean-chicken chowder. How many combinations can you come up with?

Create an advertisement for your favorite new recipe and draw a picture of your creation.

REARRANGE

Teacher's Overview

NAME OF TOOL: Rearrange

DEFINITION: Move things around; place parts in a different order; adapt.

DESCRIPTION: Sometimes we already have everything needed to solve a problem, but the parts of the solution aren't arranged properly. By rearranging these components into a different sequence, we can find a solution. As an example, when Eli Whitney wanted to build rifles for the US Army, guns were generally made one at a time by skilled craftsmen. By rearranging the tasks associated with manufacturing, Whitney enabled each worker to master just one task and do it repetitively. This allowed guns to be made by semi-skilled labor; it also guaranteed that the various parts were interchangeable. This "rearrangment" of labor resulted in the new system of mass production.

APPLICATIONS

1. You've decided to rearrange your classroom. Draw a model of the classroom as it is now. Next, draw a new model of the classroom showing how you'd like it to be arranged. What things were moved? Why? Whose desks were rearranged? Why? Which arrangement do you like best? Why?

2. You have been informed that you must rearrange your closet to make room for your younger brother or sister who will be sharing it with you. List all the ideas you can think of for rearranging your closet. Draw a "before" and "after" picture.

3. A local TV station has a show called "Here's Looking at You." Each week the producers select as a guest someone from the community. To be considered, you have to write them a letter. You really want to be on this show. Using complete sentences, list six things that are special about you that would impress the producers. Look at your list. Try rearranging the sentences to see if you can make a greater impact. (Hint: Do you want to hit your strongest point first? Or start more slowly and build to a climax?) When you have found the best order, write your letter to the producers. Remember to really sell yourself!

4. You are the president of a business and some of your employees want to start work at different hours. How do you feel about this? What kinds of things do you need to consider when allowing people to change their schedules? What suggestions would you have for your employees to make rescheduling work for everyone?

5. As an interior decorator, you've been chosen to change the layout of furniture in someone's home. How would you arrange the furniture in a living room to make the room appear larger? How would you arrange the furniture to make the room appear smaller? Using your home as an example, draw a picture showing the furniture as it is arranged today. Next, show an arrangement that would make the room seem bigger. Then draw an arrangement that makes the room appear smaller.

6. You are a parent who works every day and takes your children to school. Today you must take your baby to the doctor, too. What kinds of things could you do to rearrange your routine to get everything done? List as many ideas as you can. Make a cartoon with three or four frames showing your favorite solution.

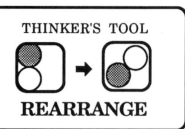

THINKER'S TOOL

REARRANGE

You've decided to rearrange your classroom.
Draw a model of the classroom as it is now.

Next, draw a new model of the classroom showing how you'd like it to be arranged.

What things were moved? Why?

Whose desks were rearranged? Why?

Which arrangement do you like best? Why?

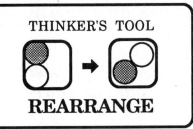

THINKER'S TOOL

REARRANGE

You have been informed that you must rearrange your closet to make room for your younger brother or sister who will be sharing it with you. List all the ideas you can think of for rearranging your closet.

Draw a "before" and "after" picture.

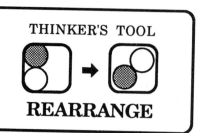

THINKER'S TOOL

REARRANGE

A local TV station has a show called "Here's Looking at You." Each week the producers select as a guest someone from the community. To be considered, you have to write them a letter. You really want to be on this show. Using complete sentences, list six things that are special about you that would impress the producers.

Look at your list. Try rearranging the sentences to see if you can make a greater impact. (Hint: Do you want to hit your strongest point first? Or start more slowly and build to a climax?)

When you have found the best order, write your letter to the producers. Remember to really sell yourself!

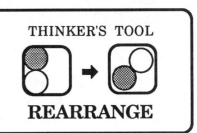

THINKER'S TOOL

REARRANGE

You are the president of a business and some of your employees want to start work at different hours. How do you feel about this?

What kinds of things do you need to consider when allowing people to change their schedules?

What suggestions would you have for your employees to make rescheduling work for everyone?

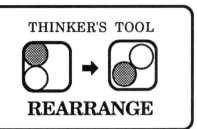

As an interior decorator, you've been chosen to change the layout of furniture in someone's home. How would you arrange the furniture in a living room to make the room appear larger?

How would you arrange the furniture to make the room appear smaller?

Using your home as an example, draw a picture showing the furniture as it is arranged today. Next, show an arrangement that would make the room seem bigger. Then draw an arrangement that makes the room appear smaller.

THINKER'S TOOL

REARRANGE

You are a parent who works every day and takes your children to school. Today you must take your baby to the doctor, too. What kinds of things could you do to rearrange your routine to get everything done? List as many ideas as you can.

Make a cartoon with three or four frames showing your favorite solution.

CLASSIFY

Teacher's Overview

NAME OF TOOL: Classify

DEFINITION: Group, sort, or categorize objects, ideas, people.

DESCRIPTION: Sometimes we can find solutions by classifying elements of a problem to look for similarities to other problems we may have solved in the past. The ability to identify attributes and to group like things together can be very helpful. Scientific researchers may find that their colleagues in a different field have solved problems similar to the ones they themselves are working on. Unfortunately, such people often remain unaware of each other's work for years because no one takes the time to classify the common aspects of their work.

APPLICATIONS

1. Classify the objects in your classroom:
- What things are round?
- What things are oval?
- What things are square?
- What things are rectangular?
- What other shapes are present in the room?

Count the objects in each category and make a graph to show the results. In what other ways could you classify the objects in your classroom?

2. Classify (group) your classmates by hair color, eye color, and whether they have brothers or sisters. Add another attribute of your choice. Graph your results.

3. Bring a collection of rocks, stamps, buttons, or other small objects to school and classify them according to shapes, colors, textures, sizes, and so on.

4. You are working for a grocery store and you are asked to sort the fruit for display. Should the bananas that are over-ripe be classified (grouped) apart from the others? What about oranges and tangerines—should they be grouped separately or together? Draw a diagram of the fruit section showing your system of classification.

5. You are a police captain who has been put in charge of a murder case. You must select a group of officers to solve this crime. What plan will you use to select these people? What personal and professional qualities make them the best people for this case?

6. You are the manager of a sports store with a large surplus of sporting goods and you want to have an end-of-the-season sale. Classify the items that should go on sale. (Hint: Think of seasonal items.) How would your sale change if it were held six months later?

Classify the objects in your classroom by shape.

• What things are round?

• What things are oval?

• What things are square?

• What things are rectangular?

• What other shapes are present in the room?

Count the objects in each category and make a graph to show the results.

In what other ways could you classify the objects in your classroom?

THINKER'S TOOL

○▲■ → ○○○
■○▲   ▲▲▲
○■▲   ■■■

CLASSIFY

Classify (group) your classmates by hair color, eye color, and whether they have brothers or sisters. Add another attribute of your choice. Graph your results.

THINKER'S TOOL

○ ▲ ▣   ○ ○ ○
▣ ○ ▲ ➡   ▲ ▲ ▲
○ ▣ ▲   ▣ ▣ ▣

CLASSIFY

Bring a collection of rocks, stamps, buttons, or
other small objects to school and classify them
according to shapes, colors, textures, sizes, and
so on.

THINKER'S TOOL

CLASSIFY

You are working for a grocery store and you are asked to sort the fruit for display. Should the bananas that are over-ripe be classified (grouped) apart from the others? What about oranges and tangerines—should they be grouped separately or together? Draw a diagram of the fruit section showing your system of classification.

THINKER'S TOOL

○ ▲ ▦   ○ ○ ○
▦ ○ ▲ ➡ ▲ ▲ ▲
○ ▦ ▲   ▦ ▦ ▦

CLASSIFY

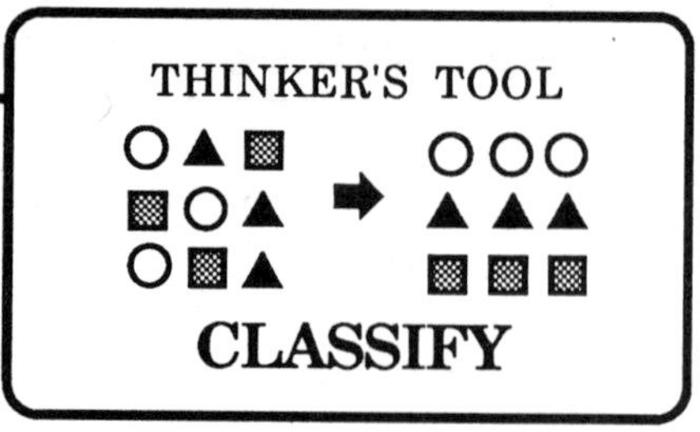

You are a police captain who has been put in charge of a murder case. You must select a group of officers to solve this crime. What plan will you use to select these people? What personal and professional qualities make them the best people for this case?

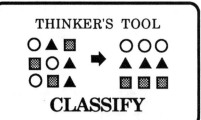

You are the manager of a sports store with a large surplus of sporting goods and you want to have an end-of-the-season sale. Classify the items that should go on sale. (Hint: Think of seasonal items.)

How would your sale change if it were held six months later?

SUBSTITUTE

Teacher's Overview

NAME OF TOOL: Substitute

DEFINITION: Put one thing in place of another.

DESCRIPTION: This tool enables us to see various options in a problem situation and helps with fluency. The creative chef who runs out of noodles doesn't panic, but simply substitutes something else and creates a new dish in the process. When materials shortages occur, creative people find adequate substitutes. Many years ago, when copper was hard to get, aluminum wire was used as a substitute for electrical wiring. Our dimes and quarters used to be made of silver. Now they are made of another material that is less expensive. George Washington Carver, the famous botanist and inventor, convinced Georgia farmers to substitute peanuts for cotton when their cotton crops were destroyed by pests. The peanut plants not only replenished the nutrients in the soil, but created new classes of products for the farmers to sell. Some of these products, like peanut oil, were promoted as substitutes for other cooking oils. Many of Carver's applications for the peanut are still in use today.

APPLICATIONS

1. Your class has planned a swim party but it starts to rain heavily that day. What can you substitute for the swim party? List as many possibilities as you can.

2. Your bike is an exact copy of your best friend's. What can you substitute on your bike so that you can tell the two apart? Draw a "before" and "after" picture. Label the changed parts on both pictures.

---

3. Most of us know the story about Christopher Columbus discovering America. How would the story change if Huckleberry Finn had been in Columbus's shoes? What if you had been Columbus? What if Martin Luther King had become president? Create your own historical substitution, write a story about it, and illustrate your story.

4. You started a fight on the playground. What actions could you have substituted to have avoided the fight? List as many as you can. Choose the best solution. Draw a picture of it.

5. You have a very important meeting to attend. When you get into your car, it won't start! What other modes of transportation could you substitute for your car? See how many you can name. Don't stop at the obvious.

6. You are having a dinner party and the flowers on the table are wilted. What could you substitute for the centerpiece? Be creative! List as many ideas as you can.

7. You are a parent who is taking ten children to the movies for your child's birthday party. When you get to the theater, you find it is closed! What activities could you substitute for the movie? See if you can list 20 different ideas. Draw a picture of your favorite solution.

THINKER'S TOOL

SUBSTITUTE

Your class has planned a swim party but it starts to rain heavily that day. What can you substitute for the swim party? List as many possibilities as you can.

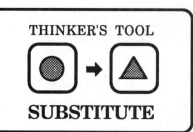

THINKER'S TOOL

SUBSTITUTE

Your bike is an exact copy of your best friend's. What can you substitute on your bike so that you can tell the two apart?

Draw a "before" and "after" picture. Label the changed parts on both pictures.

THINKER'S TOOL

SUBSTITUTE

Most of us know the story about Christopher Columbus discovering America. How would the story change if Huckleberry Finn had been in Columbus's shoes?

What if you had been Columbus?

What if Martin Luther King had become president?

Create your own historical substitution, write a story about it, and illustrate your story.

THINKER'S TOOL

SUBSTITUTE

You started a fight on the playground. What actions could you have substituted to have avoided the fight? List as many as you can.

Choose the best solution. Draw a picture of it.

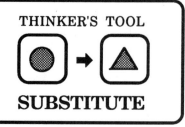

THINKER'S TOOL

SUBSTITUTE

You have a very important meeting to attend. When you get into your car, it won't start! What other modes of transportation could you substitute for your car? See how many you can name. Don't stop at the obvious.

You are having a dinner party and the flowers on the table are wilted. What could you substitute for the centerpiece? Be creative! List as many ideas as you can.

THINKER'S TOOL

SUBSTITUTE

You are a parent who is taking ten children to the movies for your child's birthday party. When you get to the theater, you find it is closed! What activities could you substitute for the movie? See if you can list 20 different ideas.

Draw a picture of your favorite solution.

REDUCE

Teacher's Overview

NAME OF TOOL: Reduce

DEFINITION: Decrease; lessen; miniaturize.

DESCRIPTION: Some problems can be solved by thinking small. Years ago, before the invention of miniaturized electronics, the smallest radios weighed several pounds. Even the first "portable" radios were quite bulky. Now, tiny radios can be found in watches. As another example, when the world was experiencing a shortage of oil some years back, car manufacturers started creating engines that reduced the need for fuel. This reduction in fuel consumption solved two problems: it helped conserve a natural resource, and also it lessened the production of pollutants.

APPLICATIONS

1. Your teacher has asked you to bring a returning classmate up to date on the material covered during the past week. Reduce last week's lessons to a list of the essential (most important) items that were taught during the week.

2. Your parents have just reduced your allowance. List all the ways you could make your new allowance last longer. That is, how can you reduce your spending?

3. You are throwing a party for Halloween and you want to turn your home into a haunted house. Because of your budget, you will be making all the decorations yourself. You can picture the perfect haunted house in your mind—a creaky old gray, two-story mansion

---

sitting alone on top of a hill, with a tall, scraggly old tree in front. Unfortunately, you live in a little white one-story house,with a tidy yard, on a busy street. Given this setting, how can you create the feel of a haunted house? (Hint: Think small. What little details can help create an overall effect?)

4. You are an architect who has been asked to design a museum building. Why would it be a good idea to create a small model of the museum first? List as many reasons as you can.

5. Because you feel that shoes have become too costly, you decide to design a very inexpensive shoe. First list all the essential parts of a shoe. Are there any ways that one part can be made to serve two functions? Can you make a shoe from one piece of material? What materials could you use? Make a drawing of your design and label all the parts.

6. You are an architect who has designed a new office building. Your boss has just told you that your design is too expensive to build. What kinds of things could you take out of a fancy office building to make it less expensive to construct? Draw a "before" and "after" picture.

THINKER'S TOOL

REDUCE

Your teacher has asked you to bring a returning classmate up to date on the material covered during the past week. Reduce last week's lessons to a list of the essential (most important) items that were taught during the week.

Your parents have just reduced your allowance. List all the ways you could make your new allowance last longer. That is, how can you reduce your spending?

Using a Tool from the Thinker's Toolbox

THINKER'S TOOL

REDUCE

You are throwing a party for Halloween and you want to turn your home into a haunted house. Because of your budget, you will be making all the decorations yourself. You can picture the perfect haunted house in your mind—a creaky old gray, two-story mansion sitting alone on top of a hill, with a tall, scraggly old tree in front.

Unfortunately, you live in a little white one-story house, with a tidy yard, on a busy street. Given this setting, how can you create the feel of a haunted house? (Hint: Think small. What little details can help create an overall effect?)

THINKER'S TOOL

REDUCE

You are an architect who has been asked to design a museum building. Why would it be a good idea to create a small model of the museum first? List as many reasons as you can.

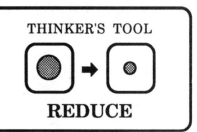

THINKER'S TOOL

REDUCE

Because you feel that shoes have become too costly, you decide to design a very inexpensive shoe. First list all the essential parts of a shoe.

Are there any ways that one part can be made to serve two functions? Can you make a shoe from one piece of material? What materials could you use? Make a drawing of your design and label all the parts.

THINKER'S TOOL

REDUCE

You are an architect who has designed a new office building. Your boss has just told you that your design is too expensive to build. What kinds of things could you take out of a fancy office building to make it less expensive to construct?

Draw a "before" and "after" picture.

EXAGGERATE

Teacher's Overview

NAME OF TOOL: Exaggerate

DEFINITION: Overstate; blow up; make outrageous; stretch the point; make bigger.

DESCRIPTION: Exaggerating features is a technique often used in design. For example, to give a new look to fashionable clothes, the designer may exaggerate the shoulder pads or lapels. Push-button telephones with very large buttons were devised specifically to help people with impaired vision. Cartoonists exaggerate the features and movements of their characters to make us laugh. Advertisers often use exaggeration to call attention to something about a product.

APPLICATIONS

1. Your school is having a carnival. To encourage people to come, you plan to create posters that exaggerate the carnival, making it appear as big as possible. Make a list of words you could use to exaggerate each part of the carnival—the exhibits, the games, the rides, the contests, the refreshments, and so on.

Do advertisers ever do this? Explain how. Bring in an example from a magazine.

2. A scout troop is going on an overnight trip. Scott wants to convince his parents to let him go, using exaggeration as a tool. Make a list of arguments that he could use to exaggerate the situation. (Lying doesn't count!) Turn this into a cartoon story or a skit.

3. You are a clothes designer, and to attract attention in the fashion world you decide to use exaggeration. Make a list of exaggerated designs that you could incorporate into a dress, a suit, or another item of your choice; for example, huge sleeves for a dress, or a tie that goes to the floor. Draw some of your ideas. Do you think your design would attract the kind of attention you want? Why or why not?

4. You are an advertising executive. Your latest job is to sell a new type of lawnmower. How many adjectives can you come up with that exaggerate or magnify the features of a lawnmower? Compose an ad using some of these adjectives.

Do the same for a new vacuum cleaner, a sewing machine, or another item of your choice.

ADDITIONAL ACTIVITY
Find printed ads that exaggerate, maybe claiming that a particular product is the best, or will help you the most, or will last the longest, and so on. Create a collage showing the use of exaggeration in advertising.

Your school is having a carnival. To encourage people to come, you plan to create posters that exaggerate the carnival, making it appear as big as possible. Make a list of words you could use to exaggerate each part of the carnival—the exhibits, the games, the rides, the contests, the refreshments, and so on.

Do advertisers ever do this? Explain how. Bring in an example from a magazine.

THINKER'S TOOL

EXAGGERATE

A scout troop is going on an overnight trip. Scott wants to convince his parents to let him go, using exaggeration as a tool. Make a list of arguments that he could use to exaggerate the situation. (Lying doesn't count!) Turn this into a cartoon story or a skit.

THINKER'S TOOL

EXAGGERATE

You are a clothes designer, and to attract attention in the fashion world you decide to use exaggeration. Make a list of exaggerated designs that you could incorporate into a dress, a suit, or another item of your choice; for example, huge sleeves for a dress, or a tie that goes to the floor. Draw some of your ideas.

Do you think your design would attract the kind of attention you want? Why or why not?

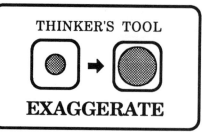

You are an advertising executive. Your latest job
is to sell a new type of lawnmower. How many
adjectives can you come up with that exaggerate
or magnify the features of a lawnmower?

Compose an ad using some of these adjectives.

Do the same for a new vacuum cleaner, a sewing machine,
or another item of your choice.

EMPATHIZE

Teacher's Overview

NAME OF TOOL: Empathize

DEFINITION: Understand; put oneself in another's place.

DESCRIPTION: This tool enables the problem solver to experience the problem from another's viewpoint. A counselor often empathizes with the client in order to understand his or her feelings and concerns. A marketing consultant will empathize with the potential customer for a new product to determine what features the customer may think are important.

APPLICATIONS

1. A new student who joined your class just today looks nervous. Can you empathize—that is, feel what this new person might be feeling? List those feelings. Based on these feelings, make a list of things that you might do to help the new student feel more at ease. Create a skit or a cartoon story about this situation.

2. Your friend has just been told by her parents that they will be moving to another state. Can you empathize with the feelings of your friend? Make a list of feelings that you think your friend might be experiencing. Can you draw some of these?

3. You are living in the 1800s in Missouri, and your family is preparing to move to California in a covered wagon. Make a list of the things you would bring with you. Make a separate list for what your parents and brother would bring. (Hint: The toys you had in the 1800s are different from the ones you have today.)

4. You are working for a marketing company. You have been asked to name a new health-food cookie made to appeal to very young children. Can you empathize with the intended consumer and come up with a list of names that little kids would like? Choose your favorite name and create an ad.

Make another list of names for cookies designed to appeal to grandparents. Try to think about the cookies from a grandparent's viewpoint. Compose an ad based on the best name you think of.

5. In your job as a marketing consultant, you have been asked to come up with a new shade of lipstick for teenage rock stars. Create a list of new colors that they would like. Put yourself in their shoes as you think about different color ideas. Create an ad using your favorite new shade from this list.

6. You are a teacher who took a class yourself recently and had a hard time learning the material. You are now more sensitive to the troubles your own students are having in class. Why? Make a list of things that you have a hard time learning. Then list the feelings you have when you are trying to learn something hard. Do you think others share the same feelings? Why or why not?

ADDITIONAL ACTIVITY

Choose an interesting article from the newspaper about a situation involving more than one person. Rewrite the article from each participant's point of view.

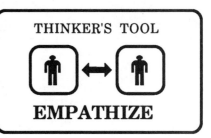

THINKER'S TOOL

EMPATHIZE

A new student who joined your class just today looks nervous. Can you empathize—that is, feel what this new person might be feeling? List those feelings.

Based on these feelings, make a list of things that you might do to help the new student feel more at ease. Create a skit or a cartoon story about this situation.

THINKER'S TOOL

EMPATHIZE

Your friend has just been told by her parents that they will be moving to another state. Can you empathize with the feelings of your friend?

Make a list of feelings that you think your friend might be experiencing.

Can you draw some of these?

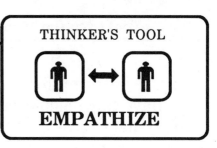

THINKER'S TOOL

EMPATHIZE

You are living in the 1800s in Missouri, and your family is preparing to move to California in a covered wagon. Make a list of the things you would bring with you. Make a separate list for what your parents and brother would bring. (Hint: The toys you had in the 1800s are different from the ones you have today.)

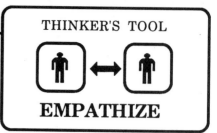

THINKER'S TOOL

EMPATHIZE

You are working for a marketing company. You have been asked to name a new health-food cookie made to appeal to very young children. Can you empathize with the intended consumer and come up with a list of names that little kids would like?

Choose your favorite name and create an ad.

Make another list of names for cookies designed to appeal to grandparents. Try to think about the cookies from a grandparent's viewpoint. Compose an ad based on the best name you think of.

THINKER'S TOOL

EMPATHIZE

In your job as a marketing consultant, you have been asked to come up with a new shade of lipstick for teenage rock stars. Create a list of new colors that they would like. Put yourself in their shoes as you think about different color ideas.

Create an ad using your favorite new shade from this list.

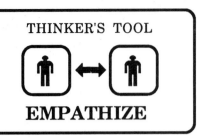

You are a teacher who took a class yourself recently and had a hard time learning the material. You are now more sensitive to the troubles your own students are having in class. Why? Make a list of things that you have a hard time learning.

List the feelings you have when you are trying to learn something hard.

Do you think others share the same feelings? Why or why not?

COMPARE

Teacher's Overview

NAME OF TOOL: Compare

DEFINITION: Contrast one thing with another; show what's different and what's alike.

DESCRIPTION: Comparing a problem with something else that may have some similarities to it often helps us see key elements that we might otherwise overlook. Many creative people have solved problems with this tool. For example, the quest for a flying machine was first satisfied by modeling one on the wing structures of birds. This resulted in the creation of working gliders. When the Wright brothers designed their first powered airplane, they benefited in turn from the designs of those gliders.

APPLICATIONS

1. To teach your younger brother about insects, you decide to compare insects to spiders. List the attributes of spiders; then list the attributes of insects. Compare the two lists. Which things are the same? Which are different? What one feature will most help your brother identify an insect? Why?

2. Your new neighbor from another state is homesick. You want to make this person feel more at home by telling about the state in which you both live now. Compare your state to the one in which your neighbor used to live. (Hint: Think about size, location, cities, industries, crops, geographical features, recreation areas, national landmarks, and so forth.) How are the two states the same? How are they different?

3. The company president has put you in charge of the selling campaign for a new soft drink, Grape Taste. What does Grape Taste look like, taste like, sound like? How does Grape Taste compare with other soft drinks on the market? List the ways it is similar to its competitors, the ways it is different, and the ways it is better. Create a magazine ad based on some of the ideas from your lists.

4. You're trying to decide whether to buy a house or an apartment. Compare the choices. What do apartments and houses have in common? What makes them different? What's your final choice? Why?

THINKER'S TOOL

COMPARE

To teach your younger brother about insects, you decide to compare insects to spiders. List the attributes of spiders; then list the attributes of insects.

SPIDERS

INSECTS

Compare the two lists. Which things are the same? Which are different?

What one feature will most help your brother identify an insect? Why?

THINKER'S TOOL

COMPARE

Your new neighbor from another state is homesick. You want to make this person feel more at home by telling about the state in which you both live now. Compare your state to the one in which your neighbor used to live. (Hint: Think about size, location, cities, industries, crops, geographical features, recreation areas, national landmarks, and so forth.)

How are the two states the same?

How are they different?

THINKER'S TOOL

COMPARE

The company president has put you in charge of the selling campaign for a new soft drink, Grape Taste. What does Grape Taste look like, taste like, sound like? How does Grape Taste compare with other soft drinks on the market? List the ways it is similar to its competitors, the ways it is different, and the ways it is better.

Create a magazine ad based on some of the ideas from your lists.

You're trying to decide whether to buy a house or an apartment. Compare the choices. What do apartments and houses have in common?

What makes them different?

What's your final choice? Why?

ASSOCIATE

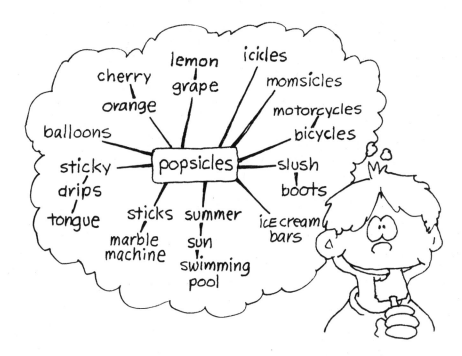

Teacher's Overview

NAME OF TOOL: Associate

DEFINITION: Pair up; relate one thing to another; form mental connections between things.

DESCRIPTION: Association is a way to release a flow of ideas from the subconscious mind. When we freely associate on a word by writing any other words that come to our mind, we often spark new ideas or insights that help us past a creative block. In the first stage of the association process it is important not to judge any of the ideas being generated, but simply to record them for judgment later on.

APPLICATIONS

1. Play the word association game. What words come to mind (write as many as possible) when you think of . . .

- Popsicles
- moon
- school
- forest
- trucks
- clouds
- Halloween
- Paris, France
- Mount Everest
- William Shakespeare
- Walt Disney
- Pacific Ocean

Note: It doesn't matter if the words you think of have any obvious connection with these words.

Compare your lists with a friend's. How many words are the same? How many are different?

2. When you think of numbers, what other numbers do you associate with . . .

- 10
- 16
- 28
- 8

- 4
- 144
- 3
- 25

Can you explain any of your associations?

Write all the words that you associate with the following numbers:

- 911
- 0
- 10
- 5

- 411
- 100
- 25
- 1,000,000

- 12
- 7
- 50
- 4

3. Think of the four seasons. Write all the words that come to mind for . . .

- spring
- summer
- fall
- winter

Are you stuck? Think about the smells, holidays, foods, clothing, weather, and activities you associate with each season. Create an ad for vacationing in one of the seasons, using ideas from your lists. Illustrate your ad.

4. The good news is that you have just inherited your uncle's crayon factory. The bad news is that it isn't making any money. You must think of a new ad campaign to help sell more crayons. What words do you associate with crayons? Make a list of these words and incorporate the best ones into your ad. Do you think your new ad will be successful? Why or why not? Using your list of associations, think of ways you could change the crayons to make them sell better. (Hint: Think of the senses.)

5. You are a senior in high school and you're writing a paper on different possible careers you might pursue. You are starting to run out of ideas, so you open a dictionary and randomly point to a word. (Do this!) What ideas can you get by associating careers with the word you've chosen? *(TEACHING NOTE: Make sure that students use the dictionary for this and that they choose words at random.)* Now pick a second word at random from the dictionary. What associations can you make by pairing these two words together? What additional careers do they suggest to you?

THINKER'S TOOL

ASSOCIATE

Play the word association game. What words come to mind (write as many as possible) when you think of . . .

- Popsicles

- Halloween

- moon

- Paris, France

- school

- Mount Everest

- forest

- William Shakespeare

- trucks

- Walt Disney

- clouds

- Pacific Ocean

Note: It doesn't matter if the words you think of have any obvious connection with these words.

Compare your lists with a friend's. How many words are the same? How many are different?

THINKER'S TOOL

ASSOCIATE

When you think of numbers, what other numbers do you associate with . . .

- 10
- 16
- 28
- 8
- 4
- 144
- 3
- 25

Can you explain any of your associations?

Write all the *words* that you associate with the following numbers:

- 911
- 0
- 10
- 5
- 411
- 100
- 25
- 1,000,000
- 12
- 7
- 50
- 4

Think of the four seasons. Write all the words that come to mind for . . .

• spring

• summer

• fall

• winter

Are you stuck? Think about the smells, holidays, foods, clothing, weather, and activities you associate with each season.

Create an ad for vacationing in one of the seasons, using ideas from your lists. Illustrate your ad.

THINKER'S TOOL

ASSOCIATE

The good news is that you have just inherited your uncle's crayon factory. The bad news is that it isn't making any money. You must think of a new ad campaign to help sell more crayons. What words do you associate with crayons? Make a list of these words and incorporate the best ones into your ad.

Do you think your new ad will be successful? Why or why not?

Using your list of associations, think of ways you could change the crayons to make them sell better. (Hint: Think of the senses.)

THINKER'S TOOL

ASSOCIATE

You are a senior in high school and you're writing a paper on different possible careers you might pursue. You are starting to run out of ideas, so you open a dictionary and randomly point to a word. (Do this!) What ideas can you get by associating careers with the word you've chosen?

Now pick a second word at random from the dictionary. What associations can you make by pairing these two words together? What additional careers do they suggest to you?

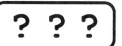

HYPOTHESIZE

Teacher's Overview

NAME OF TOOL: Hypothesize

DEFINITION: Assume, suppose; make a good guess based on some knowledge, aware that it won't always turn out to be true.

DESCRIPTION: Often when we find a problem hard to solve, we can make it easier by standing back from it and examining the underlying assumptions. By creating hypotheses about the problem, we can identify erroneous assumptions that limit our range of solutions. For example, in the early days of the space industry, an engineer questioned the need for expensive shock absorbers used to cushion the opening of solar panels after launch. By hypothesizing that such shock absorbers weren't needed, and by verifying this hypothesis with experiments, he was able to solve a million dollar problem and keep a project on schedule.

APPLICATIONS

1. Your school mascot is the bulldog, and you have decided that your school needs a live bulldog to increase school spirit. Hypothesize the reactions of the principal, of teachers, of parents, and of the other students. Do you think your school is likely to get the bulldog? Why or why not? What other alternatives are there?

2. You feel that your school needs a new drinking fountain. As the person in charge of the school snack bar, you have decided to increase the prices of ice cream bars, peanuts, and other items by 5 cents each to raise money for the fountain. Hypothesize the reaction of the students. What if the prices were raised by 25 cents? What if

---

the extra money were applied to the purchase of sports equipment for the school? *(TEACHING NOTE: This is a good brainstorming exercise for a whole-class activity or for small groups. If you work with small groups, plan to meet as a class to compare the different group results.)*

3. As school principal, you have been told that your students aren't learning enough each year. You decide to announce that classes will be held Monday through Saturday for the rest of the year. What can you hypothesize about the reaction from the students? How could you find out if your hypothesis was correct? What measures could you take as a result of this student reaction?

4. You are a naturalist deeply interested in wildflowers. While you are hiking through the national recreation area near your home, you are excited to find a strange new flower. Consulting your field guides, you discover that this plant grows only in a remote rainforest in South America. What hypothesis can you make to account for your discovery of this plant? Can you think of an alternative hypothesis? How could you find out if either of your hypotheses is correct?

5. As chairman of the local energy commission, you are facing a power-supply crisis and consider turning off all the electric power for one week. Hypothesize what would happen. How would this affect home life, school life, the government, recreation, restaurants? Why? Would you be able to prove your hypotheses? Write a story about how you would live without electric power for a week. Illustrate your story.

Your school mascot is the bulldog, and you have decided that your school needs a live bulldog to increase school spirit. Hypothesize the reactions of the principal, of teachers, of parents, and of the other students.

Do you think your school is likely to get the bulldog? Why or why not? What other alternatives are there?

You feel that your school needs a new drinking fountain. As the person in charge of the school snack bar, you have decided to increase the prices of ice cream bars, peanuts, and other items by 5 cents each to raise money for the fountain. Hypothesize the reaction of the students.

What if the prices were raised by 25 cents?

What if the extra money were applied to the purchase of sports equipment for the school?

THINKER'S TOOL

? ? ?

HYPOTHESIZE

As school principal, you have been told that your students aren't learning enough each year. You decide to announce that classes will be held Monday through Saturday for the rest of the year. What can you hypothesize about the reaction from the students?

How could you find out if your hypothesis was correct?

What measures could you take as a result of this student reaction?

THINKER'S TOOL

? ? ?

HYPOTHESIZE

You are a naturalist deeply interested in wildflowers. While you are hiking through the national recreation area near your home, you are excited to find a strange new flower. Consulting your field guides, you discover that this plant grows only in a remote rainforest in South America. What hypothesis can you make to account for your discovery of this plant?

Can you think of an alternative hypothesis?

How could you find out if either of your hypotheses is correct?

THINKER'S TOOL

? ? ?

HYPOTHESIZE

As chairman of the local energy commission, you are facing a power-supply crisis and consider turning off all the electric power for one week. Hypothesize what would happen. How would this affect home life, school life, the government, recreation, restaurants? Why?

Would you be able to prove your hypotheses?

Write a story about how you would live without electric power for a week. Illustrate your story.

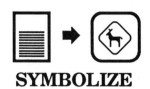

SYMBOLIZE

Teacher's Overview

NAME OF TOOL: Symbolize

DEFINITION: Represent; stand for, bring to mind.

DESCRIPTION: Symbolism is a way of solving problems in communication. With a single well-chosen visual symbol, we can convey a wealth of complex information. International symbols help overcome language difficulties. Businesses rely on their corporate logos not just to tell us who they are, but also to communicate the essence of what they have to offer. A simple design can sometimes evoke special reactions. Thus, when we see a pair of "golden arches," we know that a fast-food restaurant is near. But even further, we are likely to find ourselves thinking how good some French fries would taste; the logo tempts us to stop in and make a purchase.

APPLICATIONS

1. In math the symbols +, −, ×, and ÷ stand for add, subtract, multiply, and divide. Make up your own reasons why these symbols have these shapes.

Make a list of other common symbols you see every day. Describe what each one tells you. *(TEACHING NOTE: Symbols you might explore include the national flag, traffic signs and signals, uniforms, fast-food identities and other familiar logos, the skull and crossbones, Smokey the Bear.)*

2. Can you create a symbol for each of these words? A symbol is a simple picture, such as the heart that commonly symbolizes love, or the dollar sign that symbolizes money.

- toys
- friend
- music
- store
- family
- dance

Write a story using symbols in place of words. Use as many symbols as possible. Exchange your story with a friend. Can you read each other's stories without any trouble? What kinds of words are easy to symbolize? What kinds are hard?

3. In the Middle Ages, a noble family had its own heraldic emblems, displayed on a coat of arms, that symbolized the family name. Create your own personal emblems on the blank shield In the upper left corner, draw a symbol for your favorite accomplishments up to the present time. In the upper right corner, draw a symbol for what you want to achieve in the next five years. In the lower left, draw a symbol for your future career, and in the lower right, draw a symbol for pleasure activities you anticipate in the future. Color your coat of arms and write a complete description of each section.

4. As a master jeweler you decide to create a charm bracelet that symbolizes the 21st century. Make a list of your charms, describing each one and telling what it would symbolize. Draw your new charm bracelet and label it.

5. You have developed a new kind of popcorn. To market it, you need to design a popcorn bag that symbolizes how great this new popcorn is. What pictures could you use to symbolize (represent) popcorn? What else do you want the customer to know about your popcorn? For example, is it fresh? Tasty? Crunchy? Fluffy? Create symbols for the qualities that make your popcorn great.

THINKER'S TOOL

SYMBOLIZE

In math the symbols $+$, $-$, $\times$, and $\div$ stand for add, subtract, multiply, and divide. Make up your own reasons why these symbols have these shapes.

Make a list of other common symbols you see every day. Describe what each one tells you.

THINKER'S TOOL

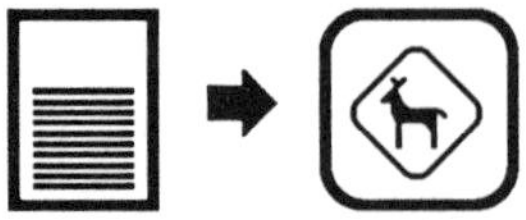

SYMBOLIZE

Can you create a symbol for each of these words? A symbol is a simple picture, such as the heart that commonly symbolizes love, or the dollar sign that symbolizes money.

• toys

• store

• friend

• family

• music

• dance

Write a story using symbols in place of words. Use as many symbols as possible. Exchange your story with a friend. Can you read each other's stories without any trouble?

What kinds of words are easy to symbolize? What kinds are hard?

In the Middle Ages, a noble family had its own heraldic emblems, displayed on a coat of arms, that symbolized the family name. Create your own personal emblems on the blank shield.

In the upper left corner, draw a symbol for your favorite accomplishments up to the present time. In the upper right corner, draw a symbol for what you want to achieve in the next five years. In the lower left, draw a symbol for your future career, and in the lower right, draw a symbol for pleasure activities you anticipate in the future.

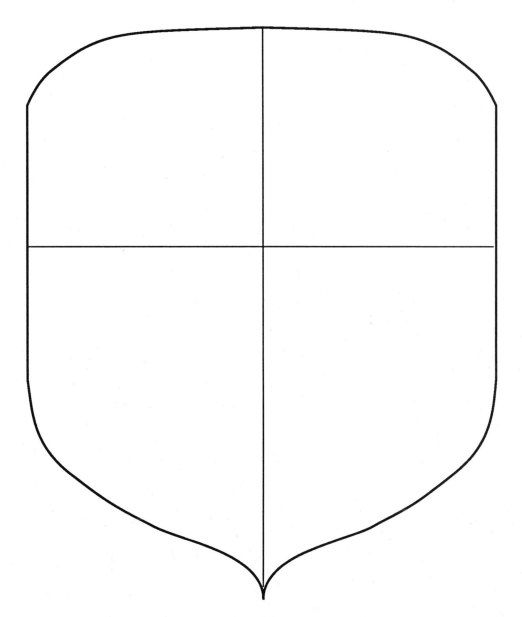

Color your coat of arms and write a complete description of each section.

THINKER'S TOOL

SYMBOLIZE

As a master jeweler you decide to create a charm bracelet that symbolizes the 21st century. Make a list of your charms, describing each one and telling what it would symbolize.

Draw your new charm bracelet and label it.

THINKER'S TOOL

SYMBOLIZE

You have developed a new kind of popcorn. To market it, you need to design a popcorn bag that symbolizes how great this new popcorn is. What pictures could you use to symbolize (represent) popcorn?

What else do you want the customer to know about your popcorn? For example, is it fresh? Tasty? Crunchy? Fluffy? Create symbols for the qualities that make your popcorn great.

SEPARATE

Teacher's Overview

NAME OF TOOL: Separate

DEFINITION: Divide; take apart; break into component parts.

DESCRIPTION: With this tool, the problem solver can get a new perspective on the problem by breaking it down into parts and looking at each part separately. This often generates novel solutions to problems. For example, when George Washington Carver successfully convinced farmers to plant peanuts, he had the challenge of coming up with applications for this crop. By separating peanuts into their various components—oils, fats, and other chemicals—he created dozens of practical inventions ranging from cooking oil to whitewash.

APPLICATIONS

1. Your teacher has just assigned you the task of writing a four-page research paper about your favorite animal. If you separate (divide) this assignment into parts, the task won't seem so enormous. How can you do this? Choose an animal first, then separate into sections the things you might research and write about; for example, habitat, foods, physical characteristics, and so forth.

Repeat this process for another assignment, such as learning the times tables, or the state capitals, or some other task of your choice. Write out your plan.

2. You've just taken on a new paper route and are overwhelmed by the number of addresses you must memorize. You decide to separate the addresses into sections to make this job easier. What criteria will you use to separate them?

---

3. You are in charge of an ad campaign for a new brand of lemonade. Where do you start? Instead of thinking about the lemonade overall, start by listing all the separate things you might mention when telling someone how great it is; for example, price, flavor, ease of preparation, health benefits, and so on. Choose the items that you think are most important and design an advertisement stressing these.

Repeat this process for a new brand of toothpaste or item of your choice.

4. You have inherited your Uncle Fritz's old car, but because of pollution, cars have been banned. Now the car just sits around taking up room. Suppose you broke it down. Could you sell the parts or use them yourself for other purposes? List your ideas for recycling Uncle Fritz's car.

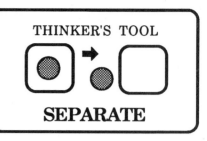

THINKER'S TOOL

SEPARATE

Your teacher has just assigned you the task of writing a four-page research paper about your favorite animal. If you separate (divide) this assignment into parts, the task won't seem so enormous. How can you do this?

Choose an animal first, then separate into sections the things you might research and write about; for example, habitat, foods, physical characteristics, and so forth.

Repeat this process for another assignment, such as learning the times tables, or the state capitals, or some other task of your choice. Write out your plan.

THINKER'S TOOL

SEPARATE

You've just taken on a new paper route and are overwhelmed by the number of addresses you must memorize. You decide to separate the addresses into sections to make this job easier. What criteria will you use to separate them?

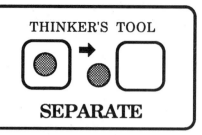

THINKER'S TOOL

SEPARATE

You are in charge of an ad campaign for a new brand of lemonade. Where do you start? Instead of thinking about the lemonade overall, start by listing all the separate things you might mention when telling someone how great it is; for example, price, flavor, ease of preparation, health benefits, and so on.

Choose the items that you think are most important and design an advertisement stressing these.

Repeat this process for a new brand of toothpaste or item of your choice.

THINKER'S TOOL

SEPARATE

You have inherited your Uncle Fritz's old car, but because of pollution, cars have been banned. Now the car just sits around taking up room. Suppose you broke it down. Could you sell the parts or use them yourself for other purposes? List your ideas for recycling Uncle Fritz's car.

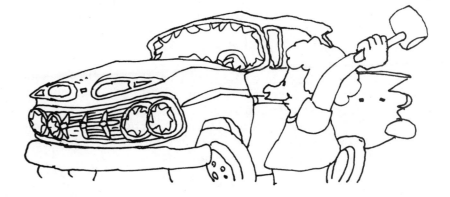

REVERSE

Teacher's Overview

NAME OF TOOL: Reverse

DEFINITION: Make opposite; turn backwards; reflect as if in a mirror.

DESCRIPTION: Sometimes we can solve problems by reversing some of the elements or assumptions. For example, architects designing housing clusters will often use a few basic floor plans and then reverse the layouts in some of the houses to provide more variations. Reversible jackets were designed to allow one coat to have two completely different appearances. Many difficult math problems can be solved by guessing at the answer and working backwards.

APPLICATIONS

1. Your parents have asked you to help think of a name for the new baby in your home. List all the possible names that you like. Pair them for a first and middle name, then try reversing each pair. Which is your favorite? (Hint: When deciding, reading them aloud helps.)

2. You've grown tired of the same old playground games. Think of a game you enjoy and reverse it. For example, in 4-square, you could change the game so the person who gets out the most is the winner. Write out the new rules. Try your new game on the playground. Did it work? Describe how it worked.

3. You want to write a funny play for children. You decide to try a mixed-up version of a familiar tale, such as "The Three Bears," "Little Red Riding Hood," "Cinderella," or "The Gingerbread Man." Choose any familiar tale and try reversing some element in it. Describe your ideas for a mixed-up tale. Why does reversing something in the story make it funny?

4. A palindrome is a number, word, or phrase that, when reversed, still reads the same. For example, "Madam, I'm Adam." How many verbal palindromes can you think of? Start with single words, then try sentences. To get some ideas, take your weekly spelling words and reverse the letters. Do any of them spell new words in reverse? Try it with other simple words. For example, *stop* becomes *pots*.

5. The owner of Burgerworld asked you to come up with a new name for French fries. You gave her a list, but the names you created aren't what she had in mind. Add to the list of names below, then reverse them all to see if the reversals are any better or if they trigger other good ideas. The first reversal has been done as an example.

NEW NAMES	REVERSALS
Fried Potatoes	Potatoes Fried
Deep Fried Spuds	
Terrific Tubers	

Repeat this process to arrive at a new name for a hot dog, for raisins, for a new brand of colored pens, or for another item of your choice.

6. As a car designer you are trying to come up with some fresh ideas. You decide to see what things in the car would work as well if the standard position were reversed. For example, could the air conditioning vents be put in the back of the car instead of the front? Could the doors open inward or upward instead of outward? Design a car with reversed elements and explain how it works.

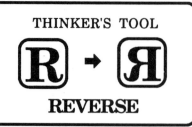

Your parents have asked you to help think of a name for the new baby in your home. List all the possible names that you like. Pair them for a first and middle name, then try reversing each pair.

Which is your favorite? (Hint: When deciding, reading them aloud helps.)

THINKER'S TOOL

REVERSE

You've grown tired of the same old playground games. Think of a game you enjoy and reverse it. For example, in 4-square, you could change the game so the person who gets out the most is the winner. Write out the new rules.

Try your new game on the playground. Did it work? Describe how it worked.

THINKER'S TOOL

R → **Я**

REVERSE

You want to write a funny play for children. You decide to try a mixed-up version of a familiar tale, such as "The Three Bears," "Little Red Riding Hood," "Cinderella," or "The Gingerbread Man." Choose any familiar tale and try reversing some element in it. Describe your ideas for a mixed-up tale.

Why does reversing something in the story make it funny?

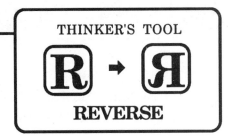

THINKER'S TOOL

R ➜ **Я**

REVERSE

A palindrome is a number, word, or phrase that, when reversed, still reads the same. For example, "Madam, I'm Adam." How many verbal palindromes can you think of?

Start with single words, then try sentences. To get some ideas, take your weekly spelling words and reverse the letters. Do any of them spell new words in reverse? Try it with other simple words. For example, *stop* becomes *pots*.

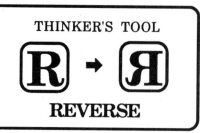

THINKER'S TOOL

REVERSE

The owner of Burgerworld asked you to come up with a new name for French fries. You gave her a list, but the names you created aren't what she had in mind.

Add to the list of names below, then reverse them all to see if the reversals are any better or if they trigger other good ideas. The first reversal has been done as an example.

NEW NAMES

- Fried Potatoes
- Deep Fried Spuds
- Terrific Tubers
-
-
-
-
-
-
-
-
-
-
-
-

REVERSALS

Potatoes Fried

Repeat this process to arrive at a new name for a hot dog, for raisins, for a new brand of colored pens, or for another item of your choice.

THINKER'S TOOL

R ➤ **Я**

REVERSE

As a car designer you are trying to come up with some fresh ideas. You decide to see what things in the car would work as well if the standard position were reversed. For example, could the air conditioning vents be put in the back of the car instead of the front? Could the doors open inward or upward instead of outward? Design a car with reversed elements and explain how it works.

PART TWO

Challenge Problems

Thinker's Toolbox Challenge Problem

TOOLS USED:

Using the Challenge Problems

For the problems on the following pages, encourage students to use the sixteen tools introduced in the preceding section. Students may apply any strategy they want and may use more than one for any given problem. You may want to duplicate and distribute the summary list (pages 136-137) for their reference. When they get stuck, let them refer to this list or to earlier worksheets to refresh their memory of the different tools. To keep them aware of their options, ask students to identify the tools they are using as they brainstorm possible solutions.

It is important to encourage the generation of as many ideas as possible. When these problems are worked as a group activity, you can do this with periodic suggestions to try thinking in a new direction. Students who are working individually or in pairs should be reminded not to hurry to a final solution, but to see how many alternative possibilities they can come up with first.

As with the applications in the preceding section, allow the students to evaluate their own ideas. Be sure that ideas are not judged prematurely. Remind students that in the initial phase of problem solving, *all* ideas are worth capturing, no matter how silly or impractical they may seem at the moment. Later on, when all the ideas have been captured on paper, the students can refine their lists and make judgments as they choose a favorite solution.

In assessing student performance, look for flexibility (lots of different ideas) as well as fluency (detailed elaboration on a single idea). If you feel a need to grade the students' work, please refer to the section on grading in the introduction to this book.

CREATING YOUR OWN MASTERS

You can select individual challenges from this section and create masters for duplication using the "Thinker's Toolbox Challenge Problem" form on the facing page. Simply duplicate the chosen problem and any accompanying illustration, then cut and paste it on a copy of the blank form. This becomes your master for duplication. Use it for student worksheets or to make an overhead transparency display for group work.

The "Thinker's Toolbox Challenge Problem" form can also be used to capture real-life problems suggested by the students themselves. For example, suppose a student finds that someone in his or her family seems to be allergic to the student's treasured pet. If you create a problem sheet based on this, the class can use their tools from *The Thinker's Toolbox* to generate alternative solutions for their classmate.

1   A trainload of eggs was delivered to you from your uncle's farm. Make a list of all the things you could do with these thousands of eggs. List as many different ideas as possible. Once you have made your list, pick your favorite solution or solutions. Explain how you arrived at your final choice.

2   A dump truck accidentally dropped a load of orange peels on your front lawn and then left. What are you going to do with these peels? List as many different ideas as possible. Once you have made your list, pick your favorite solution or solutions. Explain how you arrived at your final choice.

3   At a garage sale you bought 5000 yards (that's almost three miles) of black wool for only $3.00. List all the possibilities for using the wool. Which idea would produce the most money? Which idea would make you the happiest? Explain how you arrived at your final choice.

4   You are on a train going across the country. During your trip the train comes to a stop and you get off, thinking you've reached your destination. The train leaves before you realize that you are in the wrong state! You now have to spend the next 24 hours in a strange city. What will you do? List as many different ideas as possible. Once you have made your list, pick your favorite solution or solutions. Explain how you arrived at your final choice.

5   Create a new flavor of ice cream to represent each of the following holidays:
- New Year's Eve
- Mother's Day
- Father's Day
- Valentine's Day
- Thanksgiving

6 You see a wildcat in great distress on top of a telephone pole. There doesn't seem to be anyone else around, and you want to help the cat get down. What can you do? List as many different ideas as possible. Once you have made your list, pick your favorite solution or solutions. Explain how you arrived at your final choice.

7 You come to school on Monday morning but your teacher forgets to show up. What will you do? List as many different ideas as possible. Once you have made your list, pick your favorite solution or solutions. Explain how you arrived at your final choice.

8 While you are walking home from school, you see a 500-pound box of fresh tuna fall off a truck as it turns the corner. What will you do? List as many different ideas as possible. Once you have made your list, pick your favorite solution or solutions. Explain how you arrived at your final choice.

9 You place 25 cents in a vending machine for a sack of potato chips and 25 sacks come out. This is your lucky day! What will you do? List as many different ideas as possible. Once you have made your list, pick your favorite solution or solutions. Explain how you arrived at your final choice.

10 After attending a basketball game at night, you use your last two dimes to call your parents so they will come pick you up. While the pay phone accepts your money, the call doesn't go through. No one is left at the gym. How will you get home? List as many different ideas as possible. Once you have made your list, pick your favorite solution or solutions. Explain how you arrived at your final choice.

1 1 You've invited six people for dinner and seven people show up. You only have six table settings—plates, knives, forks, and so forth. What can you do? List as many different ideas as possible. Once you have made your list, pick your favorite solution or solutions. Explain how you arrived at your final choice.

1 2 You've just entered a soap box derby. The rules state that you must use only materials from around your own home. What can you use from your house to make your entry look different from the others? List as many different ideas as possible. Once you have made your list, pick your favorite solution or solutions. Explain how you arrived at your final choice.

1 3 Your folks have finally agreed to let you plan your own birthday party. What could you do to make your party completely different from others you have attended? List as many different ideas as possible. Once you have made your list, pick your favorite solution or solutions. Explain how you arrived at your final choice.

1 4 How many different things can you make with:
- a pen, a lemon, and a bag of popcorn?
- a calculator, a book, and a shoe?
- a desk, a candle, and a newspaper?
- some rope, a pair of pants, and a piece of wood?

List as many different ideas as possible. Once you have made your list, pick your favorite solution or solutions. Explain how you arrived at your final choice.

1 5 An ice cream truck is involved in an accident and its doors jam open. No one is hurt, but the driver can't deliver the 10,000 ice cream bars and it is a very hot day. What will you do? List as many different ideas as possible. Once you have made your list, pick your favorite solution or solutions. Explain how you arrived at your final choice.

16 List or sketch some ideas for rubber stamps that would express "the real you." Choose the one you like best, and then make it with a potato or simply draw it with markers.

17 You find a baby bird on the ground and see that the nest above is empty. What can you do? List as many different ideas as possible. Once you have made your list, pick your favorite solution or solutions. Explain how you arrived at your final choice.

18 As a prop manager for a local theater, you have to string ten soda straws together with thread. Unfortunately, you can't find a needle. How can you do this job? List as many different ideas as possible. Next, pick your favorite solution and try it out. If it doesn't work, try another.

19 While hiking in the woods, you suddenly realize that you're lost. All you have is a box of matches, a mirror, and a knife. How will you survive for one week until someone finds you? List as many different ideas as possible. Once you have made your list, pick your favorite solution or solutions. Explain how you arrived at your final choice.

20 Create your own personal secret code to send messages to your best friend. How could you disguise your message? List as many different ideas as possible. Once you have made your list, pick your favorite solution or solutions. Explain how you arrived at your final choice.

21 If you hear the ocean when you listen to a seashell, what would you hear if you listened to:

- a hubcap
- a shoe
- a milk carton
- a grocery bag

List as many sounds as possible for each noun.

22 You're stranded on an island with 50 feet of rope, five small balloons, and a book of poetry. Using these items, devise a way to get rescued. List as many different ideas as possible. Once you have made your list, pick your favorite solution or solutions. Explain how you arrived at your final choice.

23 Your parents have said you can't get a new bike for another year. What can you do to your old one to make it more exciting? List as many different ideas as possible. Once you have made your list, pick your favorite solution or solutions. Explain how you arrived at your final choice.

24 You have three pairs of roller skates and 50 feet of lumber. Using these materials, create some vehicles that could transport you to school and back. List as many different ideas as possible. Then make drawings of your favorite ideas and label the parts.

25 You are the host of a live TV talk show that reaches ten million people. Today the studio audience is packed and your guest doesn't show up. The show has just started. What do you do? List as many different ideas as possible. Once you have made your list, pick your favorite solution or solutions. Explain how you arrived at your final choice.

26 You own a neighborhood grocery store. A truck hits the power pole just outside, cutting off all your electricity. It is a hot day and without refrigeration, your frozen foods will melt. You don't want to lose all this merchandise. What can you do? List as many different ideas as possible. Once you have made your list, pick your favorite solution or solutions. Explain how you arrived at your final choice.

27 You deliver newspapers every day before breakfast. Today, you run out of papers halfway through your route. When you call the paper, they tell you that they have run out, too. What do you do? List as many different ideas as possible. Once you have made your list, pick your favorite solution or solutions. Explain how you arrived at your final choice.

28 You are taking a shower. Just as you get your body all soaped up, the water shuts off. What do you do? List as many different ideas as possible. Once you have made your list, pick your favorite solution or solutions. Explain how you arrived at your final choice.

29 You are baby-sitting for a six-month-old child in your home. When the baby starts to scream, you discover that the parents forgot to leave the baby's bottle with you. What can you do to feed this poor baby? List as many different ideas as possible. Once you have made your list, pick your favorite solution or solutions. Explain how you arrived at your final choice.

30 Your parents have left you home alone with your baby brother. He is asleep inside when you lock yourself out of the house by accident. What can you do? List as many different ideas as possible. Once you have made your list, pick your favorite solution or solutions. Explain how you arrived at your final choice.

31 You have bought an old grand piano from a second-hand store. You ask a friend who owns a truck to help you get it home. All goes well until you find that the piano won't fit through your front door. What solutions can you think of for this problem? List as many different ideas as possible. Once you have made your list, pick your favorite solution or solutions. Explain how you arrived at your final choice.

32 Take a walk outside and make a list of 50 things you see that are orange and fuzzy.

33 You have been given $100 for your birthday. You decide to use this money to start a business. What businesses could you start? Which would bring in the most money? Which would make you the happiest? Why? List as many different ideas as possible. What would be your final choice? Why?

34 Create a list of uses for the small bits of soap that are too tiny to use in the shower any longer. List as many different ideas as possible. Once you have made your list, pick your favorite solution or solutions. Explain how you arrived at your final choice.

35 Think of as many ways as possible to find your car in a large, crowded parking lot. Once you have made your list, pick your favorite solution or solutions. Explain how you arrived at your final choice.

36 What could you add to a Frisbee to make it more interesting or fun? Once you have made your list, pick your favorite solution or solutions. Explain how you arrived at your final choice.

37 Design a greeting card for each of the following holidays:
- Groundhog Day
- First Day of Spring
- Kid's Day
- First Day of School
- Last Day of School
- National Pizza Day
- National Handwriting Day
- National Failure's Day
- International Children's Book Day
- National Grouch Day
- World Hello Day
- National Nothing Day

38 Using crayons or markers, design some fancy candles. See how many completely different ideas you can come up with. Circle your favorite design and tell why you like it.

39 Design some new frames for sunglasses that represent different hobbies or foods. Choose your favorite design and write an advertisement for it. Include a picture in your ad.

40 Design different hats for all your moods. Choose your favorite design and explain why it suits the mood perfectly.

41 Design a drive-in movie theater for kids only. Describe or draw all the features that make it different from the usual drive-in.

42 Design a device that would catch a falling cat without hurting it.

43 Design a container that will hold a fresh egg and can be dropped onto the floor from a height of six feet without breaking the egg. Build your best idea and try it out.

44 Come up with a new soft drink to sell specifically in each of the following countries:
- Brazil
- France
- Germany
- Switzerland
- Iceland
- Egypt
- Samoa
- China

Design a soft-drink can for each country.

45 Design some new soft-drink containers that kids would like. Decide which one would be the best seller and explain why.

46 Design a marble dispenser that you could carry in your pocket or wear on your belt.

47 Design a pocket-sized gumball machine.

48 Design a new way to carry your books home from school.

49 Design a necklace or belt for each of the following:
- teacher
- parent
- secretary
- doctor
- school principal
- plumber

50 Design some labels for peanut butter that would appeal to kids. Choose your favorite design. Do you think it would help sell peanut butter? Why or why not?

51 You paid for two tickets for a trip to the Bahamas and the agency sent you another ticket as a surprise bonus. What will you do with it? List as many different ideas as possible. Once you have made your list, pick your favorite solution or solutions. Explain how you arrived at your final choice.

52 Design a musical instrument using common household objects such as milk cartons, paper towel tubes, rubber bands, combs, straws, string, and so forth. Draw your instrument and then build it.

53 Design a way to keep your baby brother from accidentally falling into a swimming pool.

54 You are stuck in your house during a blizzard. Fortunately, you still have electricity and water, but you are low on food. The only ingredients you have to cook with are flour, water, lemons, sugar, butter, and eggs. To raise everyone's spirits, you announce that you will prepare a full gourmet feast with appetizer, main course, beverage, and dessert. Design the recipes you will use for this meal.

55 Design a pattern for stationery to reflect such hobbies as stamp collecting, horseback riding, cooking, and so on. Make your favorite design with markers or the computer.

56 Create a self-portrait of yourself using vegetables. Use pictures of vegetables if fresh ones aren't available.

57 How many things can you make from paper towel tubes and coat hangers? List as many things as possible, then build your favorite designs.

58 Design shoelaces for teens, for parents, for grandparents, and for people your age.

59 Design the ideal pillow for reading in bed and on the floor.

Summary of Tools

ELIMINATE

Look for the essence of a problem. Some problems can be solved by eliminating inessential parts, components, or assumptions.

ELABORATE

Add new things to an existing idea. For example, add an AM/FM radio to a pocket-sized tape player.

DESCRIBE

Express the problem in words to gain new insights that clarify and help generate solutions.

COMBINE

Combine two or more known things to create something completely new.

REARRANGE

Rearrange components into a different sequence to solve a problem. For example, mass production was created by rearranging the tasks associated with manufacturing.

CLASSIFY

Classify the problem by seeing if it has any similarities to other kinds of problems you may have solved in the past.

SUBSTITUTE

Substitute one material, part, or idea for another. For example, many years ago when copper was hard to get, aluminum wire was used as a substitute for electrical wiring.

REDUCE

Examine what can be made smaller, less elaborate, more efficient.

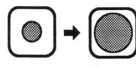

EXAGGERATE

Exaggerate features to create new solutions. For example, push-button telephones with very large buttons can be used by people with impaired vision.

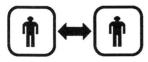

EMPATHIZE

Experience the problem from another's viewpoint. Empathize in order to understand his or her feelings or concerns.

COMPARE

Compare the problem with something that may have some similarities to it. For example, early airplanes were modeled on the wing structures of birds.

ASSOCIATE

Freely associate on a word by writing any other words that come to your mind to gain access to new ideas or insights that can help you past a creative block.

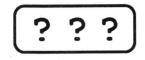

HYPOTHESIZE

Create hypotheses concerning the problem to identify assumptions that limit the range of solutions.

SYMBOLIZE

Get to the essence of a problem by thinking of a symbol that represents the task or that captures an idea with a simple picture or design.

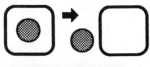

SEPARATE

Break the problem into parts and look at each part separately.

REVERSE

Reverse some of the elements or assumptions in a problem to find new solutions. For example, reversible jackets enable us to buy just one coat with two quite different appearances.

Bibliography

Adams, James L. *Conceptual Blockbusting*. San Francisco: San Francisco Book Co., 1976.

———. *The Care and Feeding of Ideas*. Reading, MA: Addison-Wesley, 1987.

Armstrong, Thomas. *In Their Own Way*. Los Angeles: J. P. Tarcher, 1987.

Arnheim, Rudolf. *Visual Thinking*. Berkeley: University of California Press, 1969.

Burns, Marilyn. *The Book of Think*. Boston: Little, Brown & Co., 1976.

Buzan, Tony. *The Brain User's Guide*. New York: E. P. Dutton, 1983.

———. *Use Both Sides of Your Brain*. New York: E. P. Dutton, 1983.

Carnow, Gary and Constance Gibson. *Prolific Thinkers' Guide*. Palo Alto, CA: Dale Seymour Publications, 1987.

de Bono, Edward. *deBono's Thinking Course*. New York: Facts on File, 1985.

———. *Lateral Thinking*. New York: Harper & Row, 1970.

de Mille, Richard. *Put Your Mother on the Ceiling*. Santa Barbara, CA: Ross-Erikson, 1981.

Gardner, Howard. *Frames of Mind: The Theory of Multiple Intelligences*. New York: Basic Books, 1983.

McKim, Robert H. *Thinking Visually*. Palo Alto, CA: Dale Seymour Publications, 1980.

Osborn, Alex F. *Applied Imagination*. New York: Charles Scribner's Sons, 1963.

Prince, George M. *The Practice of Creativity*. New York: Harper & Row, 1970.

Rico, Gabriele L. *Writing the Natural Way*. Los Angeles: J. P. Tarcher, 1983.

Thornburg, David D. *Unlocking Personal Creativity: A Course in Idea Mapping*. Los Altos, CA: Starsong Publications, 1986.

Tyler, Sydney. *Just Think*. Montara, CA: Thomas Geale Publications, 1983.